Illegal Drugs

Editor: **Cara Acred**

Independence Educational Publishers

First published by Independence
The Studio, High Green, Great Shelford
Cambridge CB22 5EG
England

British Library Cataloguing in Publication Data

Illegal drugs – (Issues today; v. 65)

1. Drugs of abuse – Juvenile literature. 2. Drug abuse – Social aspects – Juvenile literature.

I. Series II. Acred, Cara.

362.2'9-dc23

ISBN-13: 9781 86168 629 9

Acknowledgements

The publisher is grateful for permission to reproduce the following material.

While every care has been taken to trace and acknowledge copyright, the publisher tenders its apology for any accidental infringement or where copyright has proved untraceable. The publisher would be pleased to come to a suitable arrangement in any such case with the rightful owner.

Chapter One: Drugs in the UK

Overview of the UK drug scene, © 2012 DrugScope, *If someone who has taken drugs...*, © 2012 Intuition Communication Ltd., *Drugs: the facts*, © 2012 DrugScope, *Introduction to solvent and volatile substance abuse*, © 2011 Re-Solv, *What are legal highs?*, © Crown copyright 2012, *Drugs facts for young people*, © 2012 Intuition Communication Ltd.

Chapter Two: Dealing with Drugs

Young people's stories and opinions, © 2012 DrugScope, *The effects and impacts of drugs*, © 2012 Public Health Agency Northern Ireland, *Amy Winehouse's death prompts compulsory drug education in schools*, © 2012 AOL (UK) Limited, *Drug treatment in England: the road to recovery*, © National Treatment Agency for Substance Misuse, *What is addiction?*, © Crown copyright, *Drugs and the law*, © 2010, Health Promotion Substance Misuse Team Brighton & Hove.

Illustration on pages 8 and 10 are by Angelo Madrid. All illustrations, including the cover, are by Don Hatcher.

Editorial by Christina Hughes and layout by Jackie Staines, on behalf of Independence Educational Publishers.

Printed in Great Britain by MWL Print Group Ltd.

Cara Acred
Cambridge
September 2012

ISSUES today

Illegal Drugs

Contents

Chapter One: Drugs in the UK

Chapter Two: Dealing with Drugs

A resource for KS3

About Key Stage 3

Key Stage 3 refers to the first three years of secondary schooling, normally years 7, 8 and 9, during which pupils are aged between 11 and 14.

This series is also suitable for Scottish P7, S1 and S2 students.

About *Issues Today*

Issues Today is a series of resource books on contemporary social issues for Key Stage 3 pupils.

Each volume contains information from a variety of sources, including government reports and statistics, newspaper and magazine articles, surveys and polls, academic research and literature from charities and lobby groups. The information has been tailored to an 11 to 14 age group; it has been rewritten and presented in a simple, straightforward format to be accessible to Key Stage 3 pupils.

In addition, each *Issues Today* title features handy tasks and assignments based on the information contained in the book, for use in class, for homework or as a revision aid.

Issues Today can be used as a learning resource in a variety of Key Stage 3 subjects, including English, Science, History, Geography, PSHE, Citizenship, Sex and Relationships Education and Religious Education.

About this book

Illegal Drugs is the sixty-fifth volume in the *Issues Today* series.

Although the use of illegal drugs has fallen over the last ten years, it is still a serious problem. 22% of pupils aged 11 – 15 said they had used drugs at least once; 15% in the last year and 8% in the last month. But what effects do drugs have? What about the impact on our community, family and friends? This book addresses the problems surrounding illegal drugs and how they are being tackled, as well as looking at 'legal highs' and their dangers.

Illegal Drugs offers a useful overview of the many issues involved in this topic. However, at the end of each article is a URL for the relevant organisation's website, which can be visited by pupils who want to carry out further research.

Because the information in this book is gathered from a number of different sources, pupils should think about the origin of the text and critically evaluate the information that is presented. Does the source have a particular bias or agenda? Are you being presented with facts or opinions? Do you agree with the writer?

At the end of each chapter there are two pages of activities relating to the articles and issues raised in that chapter. The 'Brainstorm' questions can be done as a group or individually after reading the articles. This should prompt some ideas and lead on to further activities. Some suggestions for such activities are given under the headings 'Oral', 'Moral dilemmas', 'Research', 'Written' and 'Design' that follow the 'Brainstorm' questions.

For more information about *Issues Today* and its sister series, *Issues* (for pupils aged 14 to 18), please visit the Independence website.

www.independence.co.uk

Overview of the UK drug scene

Information from DrugScope.

People often think that drug use in the UK is out of control – that all young people take drugs and that drug dealing is spiralling out of control across Britain's playgrounds. Many claim that the facts suggest otherwise, but what is the truth?

How many people use drugs?

Of the general adult population aged 16 – 59, around ten million people, or 30%, say they have tried an illegal drug. The figure drops to around 10% for use in the last year and just over 5% for use in the last month.

For those aged 16 – 24, over 20% said they had used a drug in the last month.

For those aged 11–15, around 22% said they had used a drug at least once; 15% in the last year and 8% in the last month.

What have been the main trends in use in recent years?

For all age groups, cannabis is far and away the most popular drug, whether you are talking about a once-in-a-lifetime experiment or regular use. Cannabis use has been falling in recent years.

Overall, drug use has either fallen or remained stable in the past ten years.

The only drug that showed a significant rise in use in the late nineties and early noughties was cocaine powder.

After cannabis, cocaine has become the second drug of choice, leapfrogging over amphetamine and ecstasy.

So-called 'legal highs' (a number of which are now banned, like mephedrone) have been hitting the headlines. While use appears to be widespread, these drugs have yet to figure in official statistics so it is hard to get an idea of exactly how many people are using them. However, it seems likely that the Internet will play an increasing role in drug information, manufacture and distribution.

How much does drug use cost the UK?

The drugs that cause most harm to the individual, families and the wider community are heroin and crack. These drugs account for most of the cost of drug treatment and drug enforcement and are the drugs most likely to generate crime in order to fund drug purchase. There have been two studies – one for England and Wales and the other for Scotland. The combined estimated cost came to nearly £19 billion.

Overview of the UK drug scene

How much does the UK spend dealing with the problem?

The latest data is from 2008/09. Out of a total labelled spend of £998 million, roughly two-thirds was spent on health and one-third on enforcement, with a very small amount (about 0.4% of the budget) spent on education. However, the published figures significantly under-estimate the costs of enforcement. This is because the money spent on drug enforcement is wrapped up in the overall budget for tackling organised crime and is therefore hard to tease out. The Serious Organised Crime Agency (SOCA) has an annual budget of around £400 million.

How many people have a drug dependency?

It is estimated that there are around 400,000 people in the UK with a dependency on heroin and/or crack. Of those, around half are in contact with treatment services.

How many people die because of drugs?

In 2009, the deaths of 2,182 people in the UK were drug-related. 72% were classed as accidental poisoning or overdose, 9% were deemed to be suicide while the exact circumstances of the remaining fatalities remained unclear. Nearly 70% of drug-related deaths (around 1,400) involved heroin, methadone or similar opiate drugs.

By comparison, in 2008, just under 10,000 people died from alcohol-related diseases and over 100,000 people died from tobacco-related diseases.

How many people commit drug offences?

In 2008/09, there were nearly 300,000 recorded drug crimes in the UK, around 200,000 of which were warnings about possession of cannabis. The number of cocaine powder offences jumped 24% from the previous year.

"In 2008/09, there were nearly 300,000 recorded drug crimes in the UK."

How many drugs are seized by police and customs?

The most noticeable recent trend has been the increase in the number of cannabis plants seized, due to the number of cannabis farms discovered. Generally, it is customs who seize the largest amount of drugs in weight, while the police make the biggest number of individual seizures.

"In 2009, the deaths of 2,182 people in the UK were drug-related."

Mini glossary

Customs – *the place where officials at ports or airports check and control incoming goods and travellers as they pass through*

Dependency – *where you rely on someone or something*

Enforcement – *otherwise known as law enforcement, this refers to services such as the police*

Fatality – *death as the result of a disaster or accident*

www.drugscope.org.uk

If someone who has taken drugs...

Gets really drowsy

- Calm them and be reassuring.
- NEVER give coffee to rouse them.
- If symptoms persist, place them in the recovery position.
- Call an ambulance if necessary.

Ecstasy and speed affect the body's temperature control. If users dance energetically without taking regular breaks or keeping up fluids, there's a real danger that their bodies could overheat and dehydrate (lose too much body fluid). Warning signs include: cramps, fainting, headache or sudden tiredness.

Gets tense and panics

- Calm them and be reassuring.
- Explain that the feelings will pass.
- Steer them clear of crowds, noisy music and bright lights.
- If they start breathing very quickly, calm them down and encourage them to take long, slow breaths.

Gets too hot and dehydrates

- Move them to a cooler, quiet area (outside is often best).
- Remove excess clothing and try to cool them down.
- Encourage them to sip non-alcoholic fluids such as fruit juice and isotonic sports drinks (about a pint every hour).
- If symptoms persist call an ambulance, but make sure someone stays with them.

Becomes unconscious

- Call an ambulance.
- Place them in the recovery position.
- Check breathing. Be prepared to do mouth-to-mouth resuscitation.
- Keep them warm, but not too hot.

If you've called an ambulance and know what drugs have been taken, always tell the crew. It might save a life and you won't get into trouble.

Mini glossary

Isotonic *– isotonic drinks contain a small amount of carbohydrate and sodium which provide a small amount of extra energy*

Information from Surgery Door.

www.surgerydoor.co.uk

Drugs: the facts

Get the low down on all the major drugs.

Drug dangers

Drug use may not always be dangerous but there are still REAL risks involved.

These risks include:

- damage to health
- accidents while you are not in control of what you are doing
- taking too much in one go
- becoming dependent
- getting in with the wrong crowd
- missing school work
- falling out with family and friends
- getting into trouble with the police.

How risky is using drugs?

- It depends… you have to think about the drug itself and how it is being used.
- Different drugs carry different risks: for example you can overdose and die on heroin whereas a drug like LSD is very unlikely to cause a person's death.
- The more drugs someone takes the greater the danger: using drugs more frequently or using more at the same time increases the likelihood of ill effects.
- The way a drug is taken: injecting is by far the most dangerous way to take drugs.

Different drug types

Alcohol

The drug everyone knows. Drinking a bit is OK, but it slows down your body. Drink too much and accidents are much more likely to happen. Some people even start fighting when they are drunk.

Drinking a lot in one go can be very dangerous. People may pass out, choke on their own sick, overdose and even die. Every weekend hospitals pump the stomachs of young people who have had too much to drink.

Alcopop drinks have a lot of alcohol in them but don't even taste of alcohol. You may not realise just how much alcohol you are drinking.

Regular, heavy use can lead to addiction (alcoholism). People then feel they have to drink all the time to avoid feeling ill. Regular, heavy use can also be seriously bad news for the liver, heart, stomach and brain.

It is illegal for shops, pubs or clubs to sell alcohol to young people under 18.

Did you know that the same amount of alcohol can affect people differently? You may get drunk quicker if you are small. That's one reason why some women get drunk quicker than men.

Cannabis

The most commonly used illegal drug. Comes as green leaves or a dark brown block. Cannabis has lots of different slang names including blow, dope, draw, skunk and weed. Some types of cannabis are quite mild. Some will blow your head off. Most people who use cannabis mix it with tobacco and then smoke it.

Although it can make people feel relaxed and giggly it can also make them feel worried. They might think friends are talking about them. It can stop people from thinking clearly, make people forget things and er…er…um… make people act more slowly (like getting out of danger in time).

Some people get into a habit of smoking cannabis a lot and only feel OK when they are stoned. Smoking it for a long time might damage the lungs.

It is illegal to have, to give away or to sell cannabis.

Drugs: the facts

Cocaine

Cocaine is a white powder made from the coca plant which is grown in South America. It is often called 'charlie' or 'coke' and is usually sniffed up the nose.

Crack is another type of cocaine which is usually smoked. Often called 'rocks' or 'stones'. Cocaine and crack both give a huge rush of energy and the feeling that you can do anything. But this only lasts for a few minutes. After that, users often feel very miserable. For some, the come-down is so bad they feel like killing themselves. These drugs can have very bad effects on the heart.

Some people get into taking cocaine or crack all the time just to feel OK. They need to spend huge sums of money because these drugs are very expensive to use.

It is illegal to have, to give away or to sell cocaine or crack.

Ecstasy

Ecstasy is mostly sold as tablets or capsules, sometimes with pictures on – like a bird or a fashion logo like Calvin Klein. Many tablets sold as ecstasy are not this drug at all. They could be other drugs with very different effects. It is impossible to tell what is in a tablet just by looking at it.

With ecstasy the first effect is often a rushing feeling in the head followed by feeling calm. But taking a lot can make you nervous and leave you feeling very worried.

Ecstasy can be very dangerous for people who have any sort of heart or blood problem or epilepsy. Several young people have died using ecstasy in this country.

Drinking water and soft drinks can save lives but drinking too much water can itself be very dangerous. Drinking alcohol can make things a lot worse.

No one really knows what effects ecstasy may have on a person's health if they use it for a long time. Some experts are worried that it could cause brain damage.

It is illegal to have, to give away or to sell ecstasy.

Heroin

Also know as brown, junk, H or skag. It's a brown or grey powder made from the opium poppy which is grown in other countries. Heroin can be smoked but is often injected. It makes people sleepy and 'spaced out'. It can also make them feel very sick. Regular users often become dependent. Trying to stop using heroin can be very difficult.

It is illegal to have, to give away or to sell heroin.

LSD

LSD is also known as acid, tabs or trips. It comes as small squares of blotting paper with different designs on. LSD is often named after these designs like Bart Simpson or Strawbs.

LSD is a very powerful drug. It only takes a tiny amount to have a strong effect. LSD sends people on a trip where they will see and hear things very differently from normal. What a trip is like depends on how the person feels at the time. A bad trip can be very scary and it can make people feel worried, panicky and think that they are going mad. This is most likely to happen if the person is already feeling miserable or worried about what will happen. Trips can last up to 8 hours. Once they start there is no turning back.

It is illegal to have, to give away or to sell LSD.

Poppers

Poppers are liquids made from chemicals called nitrites and sold in small bottles with names like Rush, Locker Room and TNT. The fumes from the liquid are often sniffed up the nose.

Poppers cause a rushing feeling in the head for a short time. People often say they feel time is being slowed down. Some people get a bad headache and feel sick or just faint. Swallowing poppers can be very dangerous. Poppers can burn your skin.

It is not illegal to have poppers, but you could get into trouble for giving them away or selling them.

Information from D-world. © *2012 DrugScope*

www.drugscope-dworld.org.uk 

Introduction to solvent and volatile substance abuse

Information from Re-Solv.

What is solvent and volatile substance abuse (VSA)?

VSA is when solvents and volatile substances are inhaled through the mouth and/or nose for the sole purpose of getting a 'high'.

Volatile substances are depressants which slow down the activity of the brain and central nervous system. This results in messages to and from the brain being slowed down, affecting the physical, mental and emotional responses. But unlike other drugs, volatile substances are unique in the fact that they can also be stimulants and cause hallucinations.

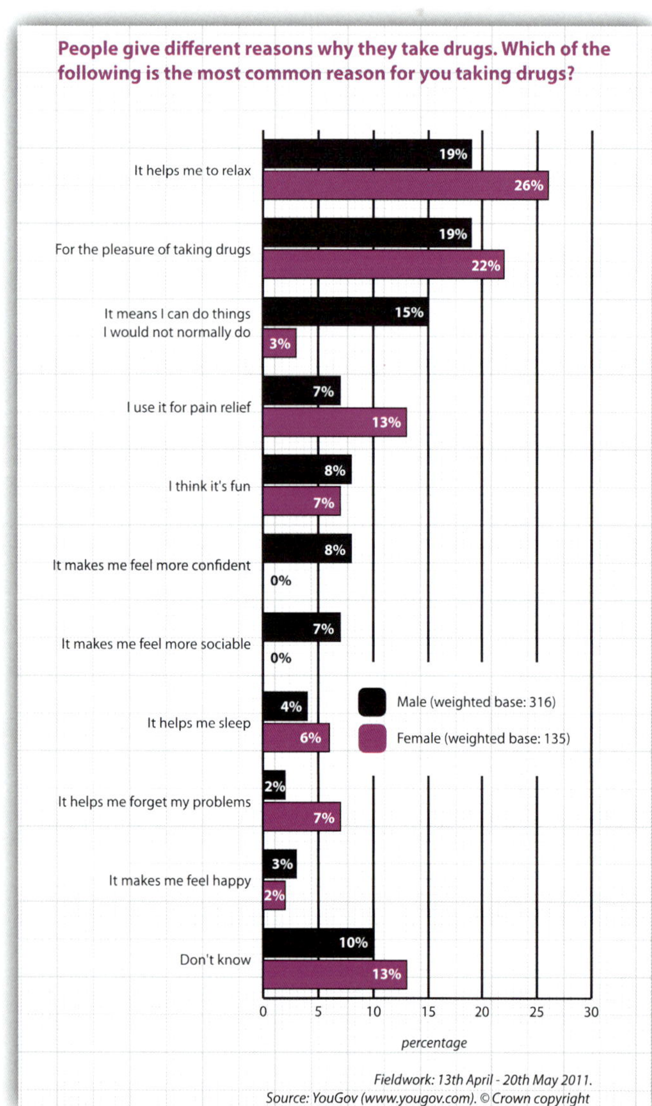

What are solvents and volatile substances?

Solvents and volatile substances are a range of products (many are everyday household items) that give off an intoxicating vapour.

There are two ingredients that are candidates for 'sniffing' – solvents and gases. They are described as volatile substances because they readily evaporate at room temperature and in doing so give off a 'sniffable' vapour.

Solvents are used to keep products dissolved until they are ready for use, e.g. to pour, spread or squirt and then to evaporate from the product quickly without a trace. This quick evaporation and volatility gives the intoxicating effect. If solvents were not used, the products would solidify in their containers.

As well as solvents being used to keep the products in a liquid state, they are also used to dissolve and liquefy materials once they have gone solid, i.e. nail varnish remover.

- Gases are fuel gases, i.e. cigarette lighter refills or propellants.
- Propellants are pressurised liquid gases used to propel the contents (deodorant, hairspray, paint, etc.) from the container. There are a number of these, but the main propellant used these days is butane.

VSA is highly dangerous. It kills more children aged 10 to 15 than all illegal drugs put together.

Introduction to solvent and volatile substance abuse

There are more than 100 commercially available products that are now used to get a 'high'. In the home there may be over 30 'sniffable' products. Below are some of the products that can be 'sniffed':

- Aerosols – deodorants, hairspray, paint spray, pain-relieving spray, air freshener, fly spray, etc.
- Cigarette lighter refills.
- Solvent-based adhesives.
- Some typewriter correction fluids.
- Nail varnish and nail varnish remover.
- Dry-cleaning fluids.
- Paint thinners and paint removers.
- Fire extinguishers.
- UHT cream – whipped cream cans.
- Damp Start.
- Dyes (for shoes).
- Cleaning agents – degreasing materials, plaster remover, etc.

'Street' names

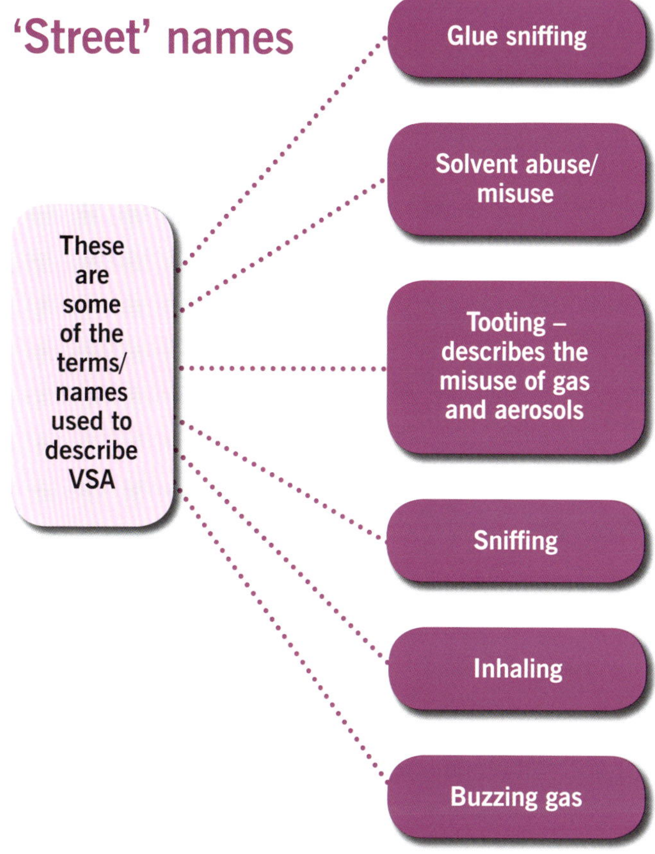

Mini glossary

Central nervous system – *the complex nerve tissues that make up the brain and spinal cord and controls body activities*

Depressant – *also referred to as 'downers', depressant drugs slow down the reflexes of the brain and body*

Intoxicating – *being overwhelmed by a chemical substance (excited or stupefied)*

Propellant – *the pressurised liquid gases used to propel the content from a container, such as hairspray or deodorant*

Volatile – *volatile substances easily change/evaporate into a gas at normal temperatures and are then inhaled*

Information from Re-Solv.

www.re-solv.org

What are legal highs?

Information from FRANK.

'Legal highs' are substances which produce the same, or similar effects, to drugs such as cocaine and ecstasy, but are not controlled under the Misuse of Drugs Act. They are, however, considered illegal under current medicines legislation to sell, supply or advertise for 'human consumption'. To get round this sellers refer to them as research chemicals, plant food, bath crystals or pond cleaner.

In many cases, 'legal highs' have been designed to mimic class A drugs, but are structurally different enough to avoid being classified as illegal substances under the Misuse of Drugs Act.

An example of this is mephedrone. The substance was created in a lab to mimic the effects of cocaine or ecstasy, but it had a slightly different chemical structure to both of these drugs so that it would not fall under the Misuse of Drugs Act. Subsequently the government passed legislation so that mephedrone became a controlled substance meaning it's now illegal to possess, give away or sell.

"'Legal highs' are substances which produce the same, or similar effects, to drugs such as cocaine and ecstasy."

There are a large number of 'legal highs'

- Some are known by their brand/product name, for example Benzo Fury, Ivory Wave, Eric 3, or Diablo. It's not always clear what's in these products and their contents can change regularly.
- Some are known by their chemical name, for example Dimethocaine, 5IAI, MDAT.
- Some may be known by a slang name, for example in some areas 'Bubble' is a generic name for any synthetic powder that has stimulant (amphetamine-like) effects.
- More recent 'legal highs' include methoxetamine (also called MXE, MKET or roflcoptr) and ethylphenidate.

What are legal highs?

Why is there concern about 'legal highs'?

For many 'legal highs' there has been very little or no useful research into their short, medium and long term effects on people. While this means FRANK can't always provide specific advice, there are certain key facts common to all 'legal highs':

- Just because a drug is legal to possess, it doesn't mean it's safe.
- It is becoming increasingly clear that 'legal highs' are far from harmless and can have similar health risks to drugs like cocaine, ecstasy and speed.
- Risks of 'legal highs' can include reduced inhibitions, drowsiness, excited or paranoid states, coma, seizures and death.
- These risks are increased if used with alcohol or other drugs.
- It is likely that drugs sold as a 'legal high' may contain one or more substances that are actually illegal to posses. What you may think is a legal high that you can't get in trouble for having, could be something completely different, and in fact a class B drug.

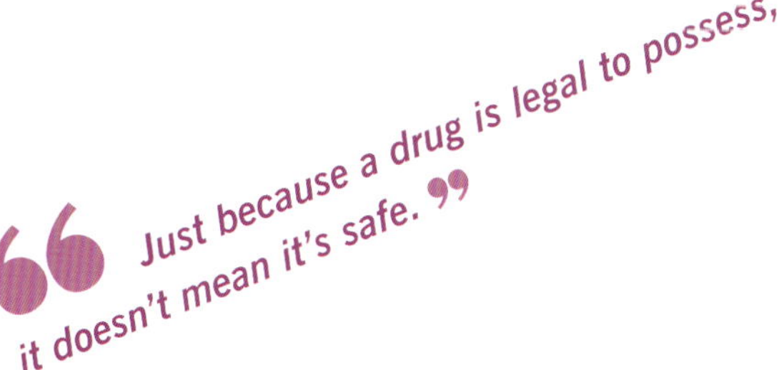

'Legal highs' and the law

Under current guidance, teachers can confiscate, and dispose of, any 'legal highs' that they find on school property, in line with the school's policy. School staff also have the power to search any students suspected of carrying banned drugs. This power allows school staff to search for substances they reasonably believe are illegal but which may, after testing, be found to be legal.

New temporary bans for 'legal highs'

The Government has now introduced new powers, meaning they can place a temporary ban on any potentially harmful substance, while they await a recommendation from the Advisory Council on the Misuse of Drugs (ACMD), an independent group of experts, on whether it should be permanently controlled under the Misuse of Drugs Act 1971.

When it is used, the temporary ban will come into immediate effect, but it will have to be agreed by Parliament within 40 days. The drug will not be class A, B, or C, but called a temporary class drug. It would not be illegal to posses a temporary class drug for personal use, but the police could confiscate it and destroy it. It will be illegal to import, distribute and sell the drug, and anyone caught could be fined, sent to jail or both.

20 January 2012

www.talktofrank.com

Drug facts for young people

Information from Surgery Door.

Crucial questions

'What does the picture on a tab say about the trip?'

NOTHING! There is NO connection between the picture and the effects of the acid tab.

Users can experience trips differently every time. The effects depend on the user's mood, where they are and who they're with at the time.

There is no way of predicting what a trip will be like.

'Is cannabis safe?'

You may have heard people say cannabis is risk free. This isn't true.

Heavy use of cannabis over a long period of time can lead to users relying on the drug as a way of relaxing and being sociable.

Heavy, long-term cannabis use can make you feel less energetic than normal. This can have a negative effect on the way you live your life.

Smoking cannabis with tobacco causes lung damage. In fact, it's reckoned that smoke from an unfiltered spliff carries more risks than a cigarette. However, people tend to smoke many more cigarettes than spliffs.

Drug facts for young people

'What are the long term effects of taking ecstasy?'

Basically no one really knows. The chemical name for ecstacy is MDMA and what we do know is that MDMA:

- dramatically affects the brain chemistry of animals;
- has also been linked to liver and kidney problems;
- heavy long-term use may increase the chance of severe depression and other mental illnesses in later life.

In many ways, ecstasy users are human guinea pigs.

'When people talk about flashbacks, what do they mean?'

LSD and Magic Mushrooms are hallucinogenic drugs – they change the way a user sees and hears things. This is called a trip. A flashback is something that:

- can happen later – days, months, even years after taking the drug;
- is a sudden memory of something from a previous trip;
- may not last long, but can seem very real. If you're doing something like crossing a road at the time it could leave you exposed to serious danger.

'Smoking and drinking aren't illegal so what's the problem?'

OK, so if you're 18 you can buy cigarettes and the pubs can sell you alcoholic drinks, but tobacco and alcohol can be abused like any drug.

Smoke and you risk cancer, heart disease and serious lung problems.

In the UK, about 13 people die every hour because of smoking-related diseases.

Drink too much alcohol and you risk damage to the heart, liver stomach and brain.

One thousand young people under 15 are admitted to hospital each year with acute alcohol intoxication. All need emergency treatment, many in intensive care.

All drugs carry risks

The effects may be unexpected.

Many drugs sold on the 'street' have been mixed with other substances, so users can never be sure what they're getting.

Users may become tolerant to some drugs (e.g. alcohol, heroin and speed). This means their bodies have become so used to the drug they need to take more to get the effect they want.

Users may overdose (take too much for their bodies to handle). With alcohol, heroin, gases, glues and aerosols an overdose can be fatal.

Emergency

Drugs affect everyone differently. Sometimes people suffer a bad reaction. If it all goes horribly wrong, don't be the one who stands back helpless.

www.surgerydoor.co.uk

Activities

Brainstorm

Brainstorm to find out what you know about illegal drugs.

1. What is a drug?

....

....

....

2. What is a legal high?

....

....

....

Oral activities

3. Read *What are legal highs?* on page 8. Imagine you are a TV news reporter who is investigating legal highs. Prepare an educational news broadcast giving information about the dangers of legal highs.

NOTES..

....

4. Write your own song, rap or poem about the different classes of drugs. For example, a rap about Class B drugs can list all the different drugs within that category and the punishments for possessing them. You might also like to mention the potential dangers of different drugs in that class.

NOTES..

....

Moral dilemmas

5. You have been invited to a big party. You really want to go, but you have heard that someone will definitely be bringing drugs to the party. All your friends still want to go and they want you to come with them. What do you do?

6. 'Cannabis should be legalised.' Debate this motion as a class, with one half arguing in favour and the other against.

Activities

Research activities

7. FRANK provides a friendly, confidential and non-judgemental service to anyone wanting help, information or advice about drugs. Visit their website (www.talktofrank.com) and explore all the services they provide. Do you think this website helps inform young people? Is it interesting and educational? What other websites offer a similar service?

CONCLUSIONS..........

Written activities

Complete the following activities in your exercise books or on a sheet of paper.

8. Write a recipe/shopping list which describes the effect of taking drugs. For example, to make cannabis, you will need 'a pinch of the giggles, a case of the munchies, a large tablespoon of paranoia'. Be as creative and inventive as you want.
9. Read *Introduction to solvent and volatile substance abuse* on page 6. Write a short news report for the local newspaper to discourage solvent and substance abuse, outlining its dangerous side-effects.

Design activities

10. Design an informative leaflet about a drug, of your choice, for your local GP's office. Your leaflet should highlight what the drug is (e.g. what it looks like, how it is taken, etc.) and the effects that it has.
11. Design a poster explaining what to do if someone who has taken drugs becomes suddenly unwell.

Young people's stories and opinions

Many people have a drug story to tell.

Liberty's story

Liberty had problems using alcohol.

'I didn't think there was a problem with it at all… and everyone was doing it. But I kind of every now and again would just do it on my own, just to kind of get the feeling. Just kind of sneak off to my room and just sit and get drunk.

It was getting to the point where if I was going out I wasn't confident unless I had a drink and I'd drink before I even went out and I'd drink to, you know, go and talk to people. I felt strange entering into a social situation unless I'd had a few drinks and … I was kind of drinking to feel normal.'

Nick's story

Nick talks about his experience using ecstasy.

'You just feel warm. You wanna kiss people. And I felt almost like a rush. Like a warm feeling that started quite low down and worked its way up my body. Arms tingling. And a feeling of euphoria – if you like. It was a fantastic feeling. An absolutely fantastic feeling. Coupled with: is this something bad that's happening to me?'

Joe's story

Joe discusses how he feels about smoking.

'[I don't] think of it as being a drug – as being addictive – you know bad for you. And yet clearly it is a drug. Yet it's so widely accepted that you'd rather not think of it as a drug.'

Young people's stories and opinions

Charlotte's story

Charlotte describes her experiences using cannabis.

'They say it's not addictive but it's psychologically addictive. All my friends did it too and we kind of got into patterns where we were telling each other, "Oh we can't sleep unless we have a spliff." and we can't do this. But that's just rubbish. It's just what you've conditioned your mind to think – that you can't do without a drug.'

Jade's story

Jade found cannabis stopped her getting things done.

'But I get up in the morning and I start puffing. The rest of my day is useless. It's just been wasted because I can't get my head round anything, even though I might have planned a very good day ahead of me.'

Matt's story

'I knew it was not for me. When I was at school, lots of my friends used to drink and smoke. A few people I knew tried drugs like cannabis and LSD, but I was never interested. I have only drunk alcohol a couple of times because I don't like the taste. But it's not just that, I just don't like the idea of being out of control and not knowing what I'm doing.

Some people think I'm boring because I don't drink, or smoke or take other drugs. But that's their problem. There's plenty of ways I enjoy myself – playing football, clubbing, computer games, going to gigs – without having to be off my head.'

Salim's story

'OK, I tried quite a few drugs when I was younger – dope, poppers, E, Acid and a bit of speed. You know things like that. I did it quite a lot for a couple of years. I was quite careful, and lucky really not to get caught by the police.

To be honest, I enjoyed it all even though I knew it was risky. Some of my friends were big drinkers and were often in a worse state than me. I was never a big drinker – I'm still not. I still have the odd bit of blow (cannabis), but I seem to be doing it less and less. I've lost interest in it.'

Information from D-World. © DrugScope

http://www.drugscope-dworld.org.uk

The effects and impacts of drugs

Information from the Public Health Agency, Northern Ireland.

Social and community harm

This is determined by the type and method of drug misuse. Examples of harm to the community include:

- theft;
- cost of police, court system, prisons, probation orders, health and personal social services;
- violence between drug users;
- poor- or under-performance at school, college or work;
- discarded needles, i.e. left in areas used by young people;
- risk of spread of HIV infection, if injecting.

Where would you recommend your friends go for drugs-related information? (all UK respondents)

Source	%
Friend or family member	33%
An independent drug info site	16%
GP	14%
Local drug service	16%
Drug user forum	9%
Telephone helpline	6%
Mixmag/Global Drug Survey	3%
Government website	3%

Base: 7,700 UK respondents. Source: Global Drug Survey for Guardian/Mixmag, *March 2012. © Guardian News & Media Ltd 2012*

Individual harm

Harm to the individual can take the form of ill health, social, personal or legal harm.

Ill health

Besides the actual nature and type of drug, the harm or risk to health can depend on:

- exactly how much is taken;
- the strength of the dose;
- how often it is taken;
- possible impurities in the drugs;
- possible mixing of drugs together;
- the person taking the drug.

Each individual will be affected in different ways by the same drug and the same amount of the drug. This is due to a number of factors, including:

- make-up of individual (e.g. physiology; personality traits; physical and mental health problems; weight; tolerance to drug; gender; family history; novice or regular user; method of use);
- method of taking the drug (e.g. injecting; smoking; eating; sniffing; swallowing);
- where the drug is taken (e.g. alone; at a party; at a club; outdoors; in the company of others).

The types of health-related harm that can be attributed to drug use include:

- accidental overdosing – physical harm or death;
- long-term excessive use – physical and mental harm;
- reaction unique to that person – physical and mental harm;
- novice use – physical and mental harm.

The nature of the physical harm can range from increased blood pressure to collapse or death. Mental harm can also range from feelings of anxiety through to acute psychotic behaviour and long-term mental illness.

Although a high proportion of those who take drugs do not come to any great harm, there is no guarantee. All drugs carry the risk of dependence.

The effects and impacts of drugs

Social and personal harm

Drug users can be viewed negatively and generally looked down upon by society. This in turn can lead to feelings of low self-esteem and difficulties with various relationships. For example:

- relationships with friends, family and employers may be harmed;
- employment prospects can be damaged by having a criminal record or by poor or non-attendance at work or training scheme;
- academic achievement and educational prospects may be harmed through poor-performance or by poor or non-attendance;
- exclusion from school or college could affect educational prospects;
- reputation may be hard to live down, leading to a person having to move.

"Drug users can be viewed negatively and generally looked down upon by society."

Legal harm

Engaging in an illegal activity such as possessing or dealing in controlled drugs can leave a person with a criminal record, imprisonment or fines and may cause difficulty in obtaining work, visas or a passport.

Reproduced with permission from the Public Health Agency, Northern Ireland.

www.publichealth.hscni.net

Amy Winehouse's death prompts compulsory drug education in schools

Information from The Huffington Post.

The death of Amy Winehouse has prompted a campaign to make drug education in schools compulsory.

The pop star 'might still be alive' if she had been educated about drugs, her father Mitch said on the eve of attending the launch of the campaign, supported by the Amy Winehouse Foundation.

An e-petition calling for effective drugs education to be part of the National Curriculum has been added to the Government's website.

The campaign wants approved drugs education and a separate drugs department, similar to that in France.

The petition, which has been launched already in the House of Commons, has been created by Maryon Stewart and Vicky Unwin, who both lost daughters as a result of drug use. Both are senior figures in the Angelus Foundation – which campaigns to highlight the dangers of 'legal highs', including alcohol. E-petitions can be considered for debate in Parliament if they get more than 100,000 signatures.

The petition says many legal highs and so-called club drugs are widely consumed by young people who regard them as safe because many are legal.

Winehouse, 61, said: 'We'll save hundreds of thousands of kids if we can do this.

'It's a disgrace that our children don't have drug education. It's preposterous.'

He added: 'We'll be saving future generations from a life of hell.'

Winehouse recently visited a rehabilitation clinic where a former addict spoke about the consequences of drugs with people currently battling the problem.

He believes that this method of educating youngsters can be effective and claimed that Amy, and the daughters of Stewart and Unwin, might still be alive if they had attended similar sessions.

He said: 'I wish that my daughter had had that kind of drug education when she was in her formative years.

'I think that had they had that education there's a good chance that all three of them would still be here today.'

Amy Winehouse was found dead in bed in her Camden flat, in July last year.

The singer battled with a drink and drugs problem during her life, prompting her father to set up the Amy Winehouse Foundation to help vulnerable youngsters in her memory.

Amy Winehouse's death prompts compulsory drug education in schools

Meanwhile, writing in *The Observer* yesterday, Unwin, whose daughter died after taking ketamine, said: 'On Wednesday March 2, 2011, our lives changed for ever.

'Our beloved 21-year-old daughter, Louise, who had everything to live for, drowned in her bath after taking an unintentional overdose of ketamine. She was not a regular drug user; she was a gregarious, popular, fun-loving girl who ... achieved more in her 21 years than most of us do in a lifetime.

'When Louise died, I knew immediately that she would want me to stop others from losing their lives in such a stupid and pointless way. I owed it to her memory and I knew that she would live on through my actions.'

Unwin said she took steps to raise awareness, posting messages on Facebook about her daughter's death, urging her friends to repost it on social networks and start a viral campaign.

Press coverage followed and as a result of one article she was contacted by Stewart, who set up the Angelus Foundation after her 21-year-old daughter Hester died from a combination of a small amount of alcohol and a half-dose of GBL, a legal high.

The Foundation has campaigned on the issues surrounding legal highs.

In her *Observer* column, Unwin said: 'In the autumn we made a breath-taking discovery: that the Coalition Government, in its recent curriculum review, had abandoned Labour's bill to make the PSHE (personal, social and health education) curriculum compulsory, including drug education.

'This means that every school can decide how much curriculum time it wants to devote to drug education (for more than 60% of schools that means one hour or less a year), what the curriculum is (one recent study found that 70% of pupils couldn't recall any drug education in their secondary school), and who delivers it (it might be the PE teacher, the school nurse and often it is a police officer or an ex-user who does an assembly).

'Most important, schools will not be measured on whether what they teach is successful or not. Research shows that drug education, poorly taught, can increase the use of drugs.

'So we decided to team up with the Amy Winehouse Foundation to launch a parents' petition to lobby government to make drug education part of the national curriculum. This campaign is being launched at the House of Commons on Monday.'

A Department for Education spokeswoman said: 'All pupils should have high-quality lessons to deal with the dangers of drug abuse. Schools have a legal responsibility to promote pupils' well-being – which should include setting out a clear drugs policy to prevent substance misuse.

'PSHE remains a compulsory part of the curriculum up to 16. Teachers know their pupils best and have the power to design their own lessons and decide what is taught. We are carrying out a detailed internal review to improve PSHE teaching and will set out next steps in due course.

'We published clear advice on drugs to schools last month setting out how they can address drug misuse – including giving accurate information through the FRANK campaign; working with charities and police to prevent it spreading and providing pupils with clear information.'

5 March 2012

Mini glossary

Compulsory – *if something is compulsory it must be done*

e-petition – *an Internet formal written request posted on website which is then signed by lots of people. It is usually addressed to an authority, such as a government*

www.huffingtonpost.co.uk

Drug treatment in England: the road to recovery

Information from the National Treatment Agency for Substance Misuse.

The use of illegal drugs in England is declining; people who need help to overcome drug dependency are getting it quicker; and more are completing their treatment and recovering.

The role of treatment

Drug workers – doctors, nurses, counsellors and others – help users overcome dependency.

They also help them to become active citizens, take responsibility for their children, earn their own living and keep a stable home. Drug users who are parents get extra support to look after their children.

While dependent users are in treatment they are less likely to use illegal drugs, to share needles and spread infections, or to steal and shoplift to fund their habit.

Research shows that crimes committed by users are halved when they are in treatment. It also indicates that most need at least three months in treatment to significantly reduce or stop their drug use.

It takes time for users to overcome addiction or manage it so they can lead normal lives. The average period in treatment is almost three years. Relapse is an ever-present risk.

Key facts

- The average wait for treatment in 2010/11 was five days, and 96% started within three weeks.
- The numbers dropping out of treatment early are falling, the proportion staying in long enough to benefit is rising.
- 28,000 adults left drug treatment free from dependency in 2010/11 – a 150% increase on the figure for 2005/06.

Facts and figures

Drug treatment in England has expanded over the past decade and is now available to anyone who needs it.

The number of adults in treatment in 2010/11 was 204,473, more than double the number in 2001. The average wait has fallen from nine weeks in 2002 to five days, and 96% start treatment within three weeks.

Numbers peaked in 2008/09 but are now falling and likely to drop below 200,000 soon. Since waiting times remain low, the decline probably reflects reduced demand rather than any shortfall in services.

Four out of five adults new to treatment either complete their programme or stay in long enough for them and society to feel the benefit.

Overall, the proportion staying in long enough to benefit is rising, the numbers leaving free from dependency are rising, and the numbers dropping out early are falling.

Successful completions more than doubled in five years to 27,969 in 2010/11. They went up by 150% compared to the figures for 2005/06, and the improvement is likely to be sustained this year.

Types of treatment

Four-fifths of adults in treatment are heroin users. The National Institute for Health and Clinical Excellence (NICE) recommends substitute prescribing as the most effective treatment for them, alongside talking therapies to change behaviour.

Some may benefit from detoxification or residential rehabilitation. A typical heroin addict can go in and out of treatment several times.

Drug treatment in England: the road to recovery

Young people (under-18s)

The number of young people using drugs is falling. Around 22,000 under-18s were helped for substance misuse problems in 2010/11. Specialist services work with young people to prevent drug and alcohol use contributing to problems later in life, and to avoid addiction.

Nine out of ten of these young people have problems primarily with cannabis and/or alcohol. This is usually a symptom rather than a cause of their vulnerability, and reflects broader problems such as family breakdown, offending, truancy, anti-social behaviour and mental illness.

Addiction to Class A drugs is rare among young people, affecting fewer than one in 20 of those being helped. So interventions for under-18s differ from the treatment offered to dependent adults.

Getting better and getting on with life

Treatment alone can only go so far. The user must want recovery and be prepared for lifestyle change. This requires support from family and friends, education and employment opportunities, and community acceptance.

The wider benefits of treatment

Treatment aims to overcome dependency and reduce the harm drugs cause to users, their families and communities.

While heroin and crack addicts are in treatment they use fewer illegal drugs and commit less crime to fund the purchase of drugs from street dealers.

Less injecting, drug litter and blood-borne viruses also mean a reduced risk to public health. The UK now has one of the lowest rates of HIV among injecting drug users in the western world, and the incidence of hepatitis C among injectors in England is one of the lowest in Europe.

Drug users are more likely to complete their recovery if they have wider support to rebuild their lives, such as support with employment and accommodation. Many rough sleepers are drug users, for example, but their drug use usually reduces when their housing problems are solved.

Mental illness is also linked to drug use, and users are more likely to recover when treatment and mental health services work together.

Drug treatment in England: the road to recovery

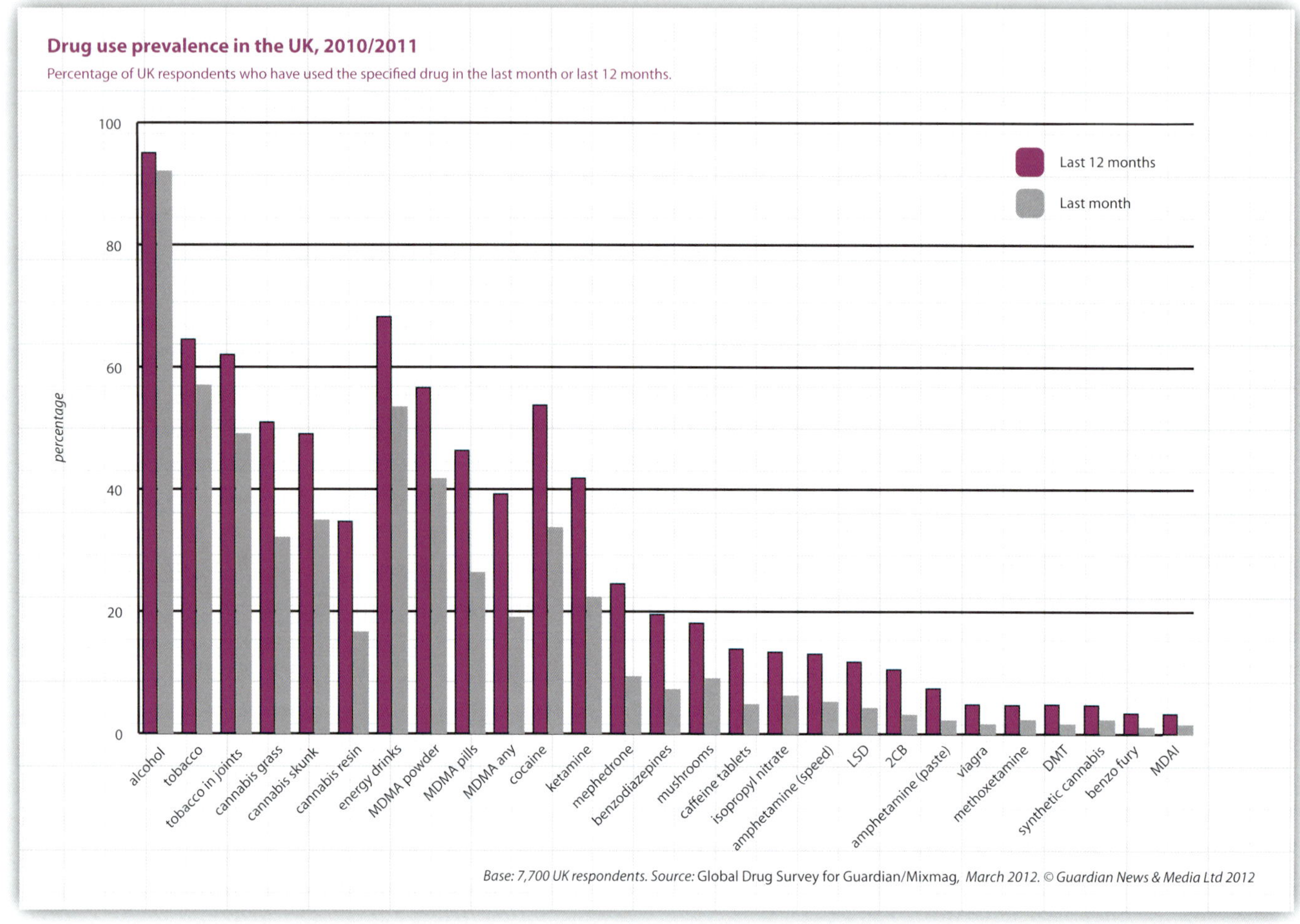

The results of treatment

- Of the 255,556 adult drug users who entered treatment for the first time between 2005 and 2011, 28% (71,887) left free of dependency and have not returned since.
- A further 33% (84,179) are still in treatment (although some may have left and subsequently returned).
- The remaining 39% (99,490) left without completing their treatment but never returned either.

February 2012

Information reproduced with kind permission from the National Treatment Agency for Substance Misuse. © National Treatment Agency for Substance Misuse

www.nta.nhs.uk

Mini glossary

Blood-borne virus – *a disease that can be spread through infected blood*

Detoxification – *removing toxic substances from the body, such as drugs*

Interventions – *getting involved by taking action to help improve a person's situation*

Rehabilitation – *helping to restore someone back to good health (e.g. easing them off drugs). Sometimes referred to as 'rehab'*

Substitute prescribing – *offering a drug addict a substitute for an illegal drug to help decrease or stop street drug use. The most common substitute drug used for the treatment of heroin addiction is methadone*

What is addiction?

Information from FRANK.

Addiction

Addiction (or dependence) is when an individual has a psychological desire to keep on using a drug even though it may be causing them harm. They may have clear cravings but they usually always find it hard to stop using. For many drugs, if you stop using after a period of regular use, you may experience unpleasant withdrawal symptoms, and this can become a cause of continued use and dependence.

Physical withdrawal symptoms will depend on which drug has been used – and whether it is depressant or stimulant. Quitting regular stimulant use tends to lead to the 'opposite' state – with for example lethargy and depression. Quitting regular depressant drug use tends to lead to the 'opposite' hyper-excitable state – for example with agitation and racing pulse. Commonly withdrawal effects can include irritability, mood changes, changes in appetite, difficulty sleeping, sweating, shaking and diarrhoea.

Are some people more likely to get addicted than others?

Addiction (dependence) can affect individuals in different ways and is very complicated. There is no test to show if an individual will become addicted. A small number of people are genetically predisposed to addictive behaviour. If they use drugs, they are more likely than others to become addicted.

However, addiction to a drug is influenced broadly by three main factors – the drug, the person and the environment. Drug factors include the drug's addictiveness, how long you've been using it and how much you normally use. Person factors include the role of genetic differences and the individual's capacity to cope with stresses. And environmental factors include availability of work and social integration.

Worried about a friend

Here's how you can help them out.

Not all drugs are addictive, but some drug users do develop a dependence. People who are dealing with addiction usually:

- Feel the need for the drug regularly.
- Have a constant supply of it.
- Have failed to stop using.
- Will do things they normally wouldn't do (such as stealing).

Sometimes people who have a problem don't think they have or refuse to believe that they are addicted or dependent. So if you think your friend has a problem and you want to help them, think about how you're going to approach it and what you're going to say. It could be a sensitive subject for them and you don't what to looking like you're nagging them. They may not listen to you at first but don't let this put you off. The best thing that you can do is to be there for them, to support and encourage them to change.

A good thing to do is keep your friend away from situations or places which might entice them – like say the pub or a mate's house. Rather, show them some other things to do to keep themselves busy.

With the proper help and support, many drug users are able to overcome their drug use before any serious harm has been done to them, or their family and friends. Other drug users have to hit rock bottom before they can see the harm and damage they are doing and start addressing their drug use.

There are a number of ways to get the information you need to help your friend. You may want to know more about the drug by exploring FRANK's A-Z of drugs, read about treatment or to find out what services are available to you locally by visiting their website And of course, you or your friend can call FRANK anytime on 0800 77 66 00 for confidential advice.

www.talktofrank.com

Drugs and the law

Information from think drink drugs.

Drugs are classified into three categories with class A having the heaviest penalties. Adults and young people are considered differently by the criminal justice system, with different penalties applying; however, any criminal record can make it difficult for you to get a job, get into college or get a visa if you want to travel abroad.

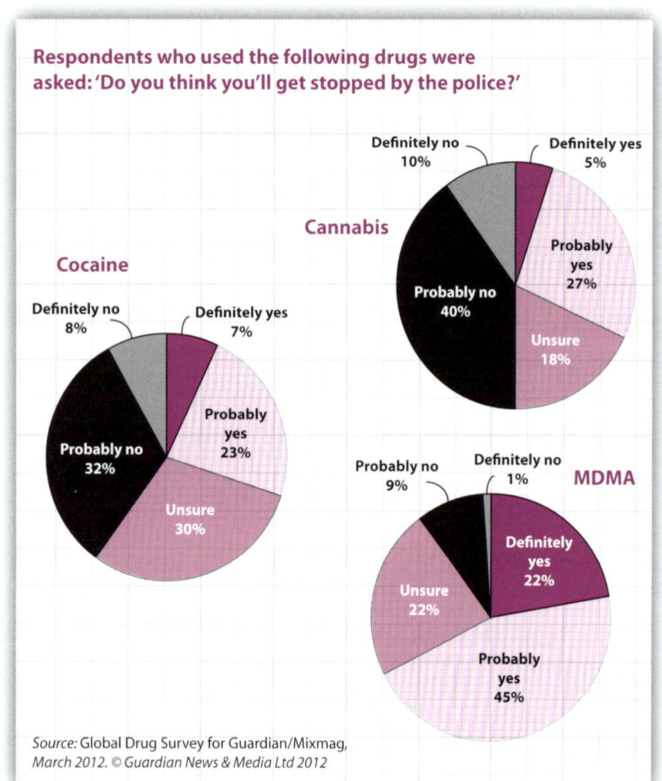

Source: Global Drug Survey for Guardian/Mixmag, *March 2012. © Guardian News & Media Ltd 2012*

THE DIFFERENCE BETWEEN POSSESSION & SUPPLY...

Possession: this is where someone is caught with drugs that they are going to use.

Supply: this is when you are caught with drugs and it looks like you have bought them to sell or supply to friends.

> ***"Any criminal record can make it difficult for you to get a job, get into college or get a visa if you want to travel abroad."***

Class	Drug	Possession	Production / Supplying
A	Cocaine, crack, ecstasy, heroin, LSD, magic mushrooms, methadone, methamphetamine, peyote, PMA, 2CB	Up to seven years in prison, or a fine, or both	Up to life in prison, or a fine, or both.
B	Amphetamine, cannabis, synthetic cannabinoids (Spice), cathinones (mephedrone), narphyrone	Up to five years in prison, or a fine, or both	Up to 14 years in prison, or a fine, or both
C	Ketamine, Piperazines (BZP), GHB, GBL, Tranquilizers, Anabolic Steroids	Up to two years in prison, or a fine, or both	Up to 14 years in prison, or a fine, or both

Drugs and the law

IT IS ILLEGAL TO...

... drink and drive.

Having a blood concentration of 80mg per 100ml or over can have the following penalties;

- up to six months in prison;
- a fine of up to £5,000 and a minimum of 12 months' disqualification (three years for a second offence within ten years);
- a criminal record.

... take drugs and drive.

This has the following penalties:

- up to six months in prison;
- a fine of up to £5,000;
- a minimum of 12 months' disqualification (three years for a second offence within ten years);
- a criminal record.

... buy or attempt to buy alcohol if you are under 18.

... to sell alcohol to anyone under 18.

Penalties include:

- a fine of £5,000;
- suspend or revoke personal licences;
- Fixed Penalty notices can be issued by the police to persons who sell alcohol to under 18s and those who buy for under 18s.

... to sell solvents to anyone under 18 or in the knowledge that they will be abused.

Mini glossary

Possession – *if you are 'charged with possession' that means you have been caught owning an illegal drug*

Supplying – *if you are 'charged with supplying' that means you have been caught giving out and selling an illegal drug*

Information from think drink drugs.

www.thinkdrinkdrugs.co.uk 

Activities

Brainstorm

Brainstorm to find out what you know about illegal drugs.

1. What types of drug treatment and recovery services are there in UK?

....

....

....

2. In terms of drugs, what is the difference between possession and supply? What are the different punishments for these crimes?

....

....

....

Oral activities

3. Is substitute prescribing a good idea? Does it work? Debate the following statement with a partner.

NOTES..

....

....

4. Role play a conversation between a school counsellor and a teenager who has been caught taking drugs at school. Suggest where the teen can go to can seek help and further advice.

NOTES..

....

....

Moral dilemma

5. You have just found out that your friend is injecting heroin. Write them a concerned email telling them how they could possibly be harming themselves and people around them, as well as how they could seek help.

Activities

Research activities

6. Research about a high-profile death associated with drug use, such as Amy Winehouse in 2011. What effect did it have? Write a summary of the tragedy and the campaign which followed.

CONCLUSIONS..........

7. Are schools doing enough to educate students about drugs and drug abuse? Using the Internet, magazines and newspapers, research different programs and schemes that have been introduced into schools to raise drug awareness.

NOTES..........

Written activities

Complete the following activities in your exercise books or on a sheet of paper.

8. Read *Liberty's story* on page 14. Write a diary entry from the point of view from a teenager, who has problems using alcohol, after an incident of binge drinking. Explore how the teenager feels, both physically and emotionally.

9. Read *Drug treatment in England: the road to recovery* on page 20. Summarise in a report the wider benefits of treatment.

Design activities

10. Draw a cartoon to be handed out at your school showing the harm that drug abuse causes, in particular the effect and impact it has on relationships with friends, family and school.

11. Design the layout for a website which will provide worried parents with information and advice about drugs. Sections can include a list of drug street names, drug side-effects or signs of drug use. Write text for at least three key sections and think of a name and logo for the site.

Key facts

- *Of the general adult population aged 16 – 59, around ten million people, or 30%, say they have tried an illegal drug. (page 1)*
- *For all age groups, cannabis is far and away the most popular drug, whether you are talking about a once-in-a-lifetime experiment or regular use. (page 1)*
- *It is estimated that there are around 400,000 people in the UK with a dependency on heroin and/or crack. (page 2)*
- *In 2009, the deaths of 2,182 people in the UK were drug-related. 72% were classed as accidental poisoning or overdose, 9% were deemed to be suicide while the exact circumstances of the remaining fatalities remained unclear. (page 2)*
- *In 2008/09, there were nearly 300,000 recorded drug crimes in the UK, around 200,000 of which were warnings about possession of cannabis. (page 2)*
- *It is illegal for shops, pubs or clubs to sell alcohol to young people under 18. (page 4)*
- *There are more than 100 commercially available products that are now used to get a 'high'. In the home there may be over 30 'sniffable' products. (page 7)*
- *In the UK, about 13 people die every hour because of smoking-related diseases. (page 11)*
- *One thousand young people under 15 are admitted to hospital each year with acute alcohol intoxication. All need emergency treatment, many in intensive care. (page 11)*
- *Many drugs sold on the 'street' have been mixed with other substances, so users can never be sure what they're getting. (page 11)*
- *E-petitions can be considered for debate in Parliament if they get more than 100,000 signatures. (page 18)*
- *One recent study found that 70% of pupils couldn't recall any drug education in their secondary school. (page 19)*
- *The number of adults in treatment in 2010/11 was 204,473, more than double the number in 2001. (page 20)*
- *28,000 adults left drug treatment free from dependency in 2010/11 – a 150% increase on the figure for 2005/06. (page 20)*
- *Around 22,000 under-18s were helped for substance misuse problems in 2010/11. (page 21)*

Glossary

Addiction – *Frequent use of a particular substance which means a person becomes dependent on it and this then makes it very difficult to stop taking it. Addiction can be physical, meaning the user's body has come to rely on the substance and will suffer negative symptoms if the substance is taken away. Addiction can also be mental (psychological), meaning the user doesn't need the substance but just thinks they do and will experience strong cravings if it is taken away.*

Dealing – *Supplying drugs to another person, usually in return for money. However, giving drugs away for free to friends is also classed as dealing and will be given the same punishment. Dealing drugs is seen as a much worse crime than having drugs on you for personal use (also known as possession) and will be dealt with more harshly.*

Depressants – *A drug that slows down vital systems of the body and makes people feel sleepy. Otherwise known as 'downers', this includes drugs such as alcohol, heroin and tranquillisers.*

Drug – *A substance that has an effect on the mind and body, which changes the way they normally function. Different drugs have different side-effects and risks. Legal drugs include alcohol, tobacco, caffeine (e.g. coffee or cola) and prescription medicines. Illegal drugs taken for recreational purposes include cannabis, cocaine and ecstasy. These illegal substances are divided into three classes – A, B and C – according to the danger they pose to the user and society.*

Hallucinogens/Hallucinogenic – *A drug that changes the way you see, hear, feel, smell or touch the world. This altered sense of reality is called a 'trip'. Common hallucinogens include LSD, ketamine and magic mushrooms.*

Legal high – *Drugs that are used and have similar effects to illegal drugs, like cannabis and cocaine, but are not against the law to possess or use. Legal highs can have the same effect as a class A drug, but due to their different chemical structure they do not fall under the Misuse of Drugs Act. Just because they are legal does not mean they are safe to take. For example, some are marked as 'not for human consumption'.*

Misuse of Drugs Act 1971 – *National drug control laws that sort illegal drugs into three different categories – classes A, B and C – based on how harmful they are to both the user and society when they are misused.*

Overdose – *This occurs when a person takes a dangerous quantity of drugs and the body cannot cope with the effects. The actual amount is different for each drug and person. An excessive dose of drugs can lead to organ failure, a coma and death.*

Rehabilitation – *Sometimes referred to as going to 'rehab', rehabilitation is the use of special treatment to help restore someone back to good health (e.g. easing a person off drugs). Rehabilitation helps people who are addicts recover from their drug addiction by teaching them new behaviours so they can live life without drugs.*

Stimulants – *A drug that speeds up activity in the brain. These 'uppers' temporarily enhance alertness and make you feel more awake.*

Withdrawal – *When a person stops using an addictive drug which they are physically dependent on they experience and suffer flu-like symptoms, making the person feel very ill.*